Original title:

The Essence of Passion

Editor: Theodor Taimla

Author: Jeannette Viirpuu

ISBN HARDBACK: 978-9916-87-020-4

ISBN PAPERBACK: 978-9916-87-021-1

Luminescent Moments

In twilight's gentle glow, we stand,
Where whispered secrets dance on sand.
The stars begin their nightly play,
As dreams like fireflies light our way.

A flicker here, a spark so bright,
Illuminates the heart's delight.
With every glance, the world expands,
Holding hope in fragile hands.

In the hush, time slows its flight,
Painting shadows with soft light.
Moments caught, forever framed,
In the gallery of love, unnamed.

Each heartbeat syncs with nature's song,
Reminding us where we belong.
Underneath the velvet skies,
We find our truth where silence lies.

So gather near, embrace the night,
Let every breath ignite the light.
For in these hours, we transcend
Luminescent moments, without end.

Passion's Paradox

In shadows deep where feelings dwell,
A heart, once free, now caught in spell.
The flame that warms can also burn,
In passion's thrum, we twist and turn.

A tender touch, a bitter bite,
Love's dual path, both dark and bright.
With every kiss, a silent vow,
In paradox, we live and bow.

The dance of souls in tempest's waltz,
Each movement sparks, igniting pulse.
Yet in the swirl, we often lose,
The self we were, the voice we choose.

We long for peace, yet crave the storm,
In tangled hearts, we find our form.
A tapestry of joy and ache,
In passion's grip, we bend, we break.

So hold me close, but let me go,
In this strange love, I learn, I grow.
For passion's paradox unfolds,
A story written in hues so bold.

Radiance in the Abyss

In the depths where silence dwells,
Shimmers of light break darkened spells.
Hope rises where shadows creep,
A glimpse of grace in the deep.

Stars waltz in the endless void,
Whispers of dreams, once destroyed.
Flickers of warmth, they ignite,
Guiding lost souls through the night.

Crystals glimmer, secrets unfold,
Stories of courage quietly told.
In darkness, a spark, so profound,
A beacon of joy can be found.

The waves of despair may crash,
But through the storm, hearts will clash.
Radiance blooms in the black,
Proving light always finds its track.

So plunge deep in the night's embrace,
Find your truth in the timeless space.
For even in sorrow's abyss,
Lies the promise of radiant bliss.

Unspoken Volcanos

Beneath the calm, a rumble brews,
Nature's fury hides in the hues.
Mountains whisper secrets untold,
In silence, a tempest bold.

Pressure mounts in the quiet night,
Fiery thoughts prepare for flight.
Unseen forces twist and churn,
In every heart, embers burn.

Steam escapes from cracks so slight,
Given form by the birth of light.
The world awaits the fierce release,
A dance of chaos, then sweet peace.

Lava flows through veins of stone,
A primal call to the heart alone.
Eruption follows deep reflection,
From the ashes, a new direction.

Words unspoken, yet loud they scream,
Like molten rock, they rise and beam.
In the stillness, courage grows,
Unleash the fire, let it chose.

Wildflower Moments

In fields of gold, wildflowers bloom,
Dancing lightly, dispelling gloom.
Each petal tells of summer's kiss,
A fleeting glimpse of simple bliss.

Bright sunbeams weave through emerald blades,
Petals soft in the gentle fades.
Nature's laughter fills the air,
Capturing hearts with every flare.

Moments stretched in twilight's grace,
Whispers shared in nature's embrace.
Every color sings a song,
In their presence, you belong.

The butterfly traces paths so free,
A reminder of life's jubilee.
These wild blooms, with stories grand,
In every crease, a world to stand.

So cherish each wildflower sight,
For they vanish with the night.
In their essence, find your way,
And let your spirit brightly play.

Heartbeat's Tapestry

Threads of time weave through our days,
Each heartbeat shapes a love ablaze.
Moments stitched with tender care,
A tapestry both rich and rare.

In laughter's echo, joy is spun,
In tears, the threads of stories run.
Colors blend in the fabric's fold,
In every stitch, a life retold.

Heartbeat whispers promise deep,
In gentle rhythms, memories keep.
Every pulse a pattern drawn,
Inwoven hopes greet every dawn.

Life's fabric pulls and stretches wide,
With every heartbeat, we abide.
A dance of moments, fierce and bright,
Creating art in day and night.

So wear your heart upon your sleeve,
In this tapestry, love believe.
For each heartbeat, a tale unfolds,
In threads of life, our story holds.

A Tryst of Souls

Beneath the silver moon's embrace,
Two souls entwined in silent space.
Whispers soft like gentle streams,
Binding hearts with quiet dreams.

Stars alight with ancient lore,
Promise forged on destiny's shore.
Hands that touch where shadows play,
In love's pure glow, they find their way.

Breath of night and sigh of dawn,
Together they weave a bond reborn.
In the stillness, they softly glide,
Across the currents, side by side.

Time stands still, a fleeting glance,
Echoes of an endless dance.
In every heartbeat, they confide,
A tryst of souls, forever tied.

Fervent Dreams

In the hush of night they soar,
Fervent dreams that yearn for more.
Colors blend in vivid light,
Chasing shadows, taking flight.

Hope ignites with a gentle spark,
Illuminating every dark.
Visions twine in whispered codes,
Guiding paths on unknown roads.

With open hearts, they dare to leap,
Into the depths where secrets keep.
Where wishes merge with thought and time,
Transforming life into a rhyme.

Awakening with dawn's bright sheen,
Fervent dreams remind them keen,
That within the heart's embrace,
Lies the courage to find their place.

Braided Hearts

In the tapestry of woven years,
Braided hearts through joy and tears.
Threads of laughter, strands of pain,
Together they rise, again, again.

Moments stitched in time's embrace,
Each a mark, each a trace.
In every fold, a story told,
Of love that's fierce, of love that's bold.

Through seasons change, the fabric grows,
Colors bright, and sometimes froze.
In silence shared, in laughter loud,
They find their strength to stand proud.

Braided dreams in twilight's glow,
Hearts entwined, they'll ever know.
That even when the world may part,
They'll remain, a woven art.

Shadows of Intensity

In the dusk, where shadows play,
Intense emotions find their way.
A flicker of light, a spark ignites,
Illuminating hushed flights.

Whispers swirl in the calm of night,
Echoing dreams, taking flight.
In every silence, they dissolve,
Mysteries the heart must solve.

Crimson hues in twilight's fold,
Painting fears both brave and bold.
Each heartbeat, a lingering sway,
Reflects the passion of the day.

In shadows deep, they learn to trust,
In moments subtle, in moments just.
With every step, they journey far,
In the shadows, they find a star.

Kaleidoscope of Affections

A swirl of colors bright,
Emotions dance in sight.
Each glance a spectrum shared,
In this moment, unprepared.

Laughter intertwines with tears,
Rich tapestry of years.
Feelings blend, a vivid hue,
In your warmth, I find my truth.

Whispers echo in the night,
Soft confessions take their flight.
Hearts beat in synchronized ways,
Lost within this vibrant maze.

Time bends, a fleeting trance,
Captured in a sacred dance.
In the kaleidoscope's embrace,
We discover our own space.

Through the lens of heart's desires,
Love ignites like gentle fires.
In this world, we brightly glow,
Together, we continue to grow.

Breathless Encounter

Underneath the silver moon,
Fate brings hearts to a tune.
Eyes lock in a silent plea,
In this moment, just you and me.

Time halts, the world fades out,
In your gaze, there's no doubt.
Our breath mingles in the air,
A connection beyond compare.

With every heartbeat, we dive,
In this rush, we feel alive.
Moments stretch, they bend and break,
In your presence, I feel awake.

A gentle brush ignites the spark,
Two souls merging in the dark.
Every second whispers grace,
In this breathless, sacred place.

Yet in the dawn, we must part,
But you linger in my heart.
A fleeting touch, forever known,
In this space, we've truly grown.

Flare of Sentiments

In the silence, sparks ignite,
Embers glow with soft delight.
Tender words take flight, a song,
In a world where we belong.

Every glance, a hidden flame,
Betwixt us, it feels the same.
Hearts alive with fervent beats,
In your arms, my spirit meets.

A dance beneath the starlit skies,
Awakens hope in hushed sighs.
Flashes of love, bright and bold,
In this warmth, our stories unfold.

Every moment feels so real,
A truth that both can feel.
Carry whispers on the breeze,
A flare of love, with such ease.

In this blaze of passion's light,
We will weather any night.
Together, a canvas of dreams,
Where love flows in quiet streams.

A Canvas of Longing

Brush strokes of a wistful heart,
Each yearning plays its part.
Colors blend in shades of blue,
As I paint a dream of you.

Canvas stretched with hopes untold,
Framed in warmth, a love to hold.
Every line, a silent plea,
In each shadow, you and me.

Wishful thoughts drift on the air,
A masterpiece, beyond compare.
Each layer holds a tender sigh,
In this world, we soar and fly.

Haunted by the quiet space,
Your essence fills, a soft embrace.
In this art of time and fate,
Every heartbeat resonates.

Longing whispers, brush in hand,
Creating dreams on shifting sand.
In this canvas, love will find,
The beauty in the intertwined.

Clockwork of Affection

In the quiet tick of night,
Hearts entwined, a sweet delight.
Every second holds a glance,
Time stands still within romance.

Whispers echo softly near,
Wrapped in warmth, we shed all fear.
Moments passed, yet always new,
In this clockwork, me and you.

Each heartbeat a gentle chime,
Rhythms dance in perfect time.
Hands held tight, we forge the way,
Love's mechanism, day by day.

Like the sun and moon in waltz,
Fate entwines, no hidden faults.
Every hour a promise true,
In this clockwork, just us two.

Through the gears, affection flows,
A treasure that forever grows.
In this wonder of design,
Always yours, forever mine.

Love's Unfathomable Sea

Beneath the waves, our secrets lie,
Whispers carried by the tide.
Endless depths, a vast embrace,
In love's ocean, I find grace.

The moonlight dances on the crest,
Guiding hearts to find their rest.
Driftwood dreams upon the shore,
With each wave, I long for more.

Tides that rise and softly fall,
In your depths, I am enthralled.
Sailing wide on currents free,
Lost in love's unfathomable sea.

Reflecting stars, the night adorned,
In your eyes, my heart is sworn.
Every splash a sweet refrain,
In this sea, I feel no pain.

When the storms of life appear,
Hold me close, dispel the fear.
Together we will brave the blue,
In love's sea, it's me and you.

Ink of Desire

Inky trails upon the page,
Every word a silent wage.
With every stroke, my heart reveals,
The depth of all our fervent feels.

Letters blend like colors bright,
Scribbled dreams take off in flight.
Passion penned in shadows deep,
In this ink, my secrets seep.

Whispers captured, thoughts unwind,
In the scribbles, love defined.
With every line, our stories grow,
A tapestry of heart, aglow.

Through the quill, emotions flow,
In written words, true feelings show.
With each page, desires burn,
In the ink, for you, I yearn.

The parchment holds what hearts proclaim,
Fires kindled, love's sweet flame.
In this journal of our plight,
Written dreams by candlelight.

Dances with Shadows

In twilight's grip, shadows play,
Silent whispers come out to stay.
Underneath the pale moon's glow,
Two hearts dance, the night we know.

Footsteps soft on cobblestone,
In this dance, we are alone.
Twirls of dreams in cool night air,
With every spin, you seem so rare.

The beat of night, a steady tune,
Guided by the watchful moon.
In this embrace, our spirits soar,
With every step, I want you more.

Through waltz of stars, we glide and weave,
In this hush, I dare believe.
Among the shadows, love takes flight,
In your arms, everything feels right.

As dawn approaches, shadows fade,
Our hearts, entwined, cannot evade.
Every moment spent with you,
In dances, our love feels brand new.

Dance of the Senses

Whispers of the morning glow,
Softest petals start to show.
Each breath a touch, a sweet caress,
In nature's arms, we find our rest.

Colors twirl in vibrant light,
A symphony of pure delight.
Every sound a gentle song,
We lose ourselves where we belong.

The taste of fruit upon our lips,
Warm laughter as the sunlight sips.
With every hug, the world dissolves,
In this embrace, true love involves.

Smells of spices in the air,
Flavors dance without a care.
Textures weave a tender tale,
In this dance, we cannot fail.

Together we sway under the stars,
No boundaries felt, no hidden scars.
In the moment, time stands still,
Forever dancing, hearts will fill.

Vibrations of Love

In the silence, whispers play,
Hearts echoing, come what may.
With every glance, a spark ignites,
A universe in shared delights.

Hands entwined, we move as one,
Beneath the moon, beneath the sun.
Velvet words and tender sighs,
In each heartbeat, a love that flies.

Every touch, electric thrill,
In this rhythm, we find our will.
Two souls dancing, intertwined,
Lost in the magic we designed.

Time is fluid, moments blend,
A story written without end.
Within our gaze, where truth is found,
Love's vibration, a sacred sound.

As dawn approaches, shadows fade,
In these moments, memories laid.
Forever dancing, come what may,
In vibrant love, we find our way.

Beneath the Surface of Emotion

Ripples dance on a silent lake,
Beneath the calm, the heart might quake.
Hidden depths where secrets lie,
Breathe the truth, let questions die.

Miles of waves crash on the shore,
Every pulse, one heartbeat more.
Through stormy skies and aching hearts,
In the stillness, love imparts.

Layers softened by gentle touch,
Vulnerability, meaning much.
In the silence, voices speak,
With every glance, the truth we seek.

Hearts like oceans, deep and wide,
In their currents, we confide.
Through the shadows, light will seep,
In our souls, a trust to keep.

Translucent truths rise like the tide,
Embrace the waves, never hide.
Through every fear, we rise above,
Beneath the surface lies our love.

Strumming the Chords of Yearning

In twilight's glow, guitars will weep,
Melodies wake from a restless sleep.
Each strum a pulse of desires clear,
Calling forth what we hold dear.

Fingers dance on strings of hope,
With notes we weave and gently cope.
A longing heart, a whispered tune,
Under the stars, beneath the moon.

Echoes linger in the night,
Yearning souls take flight in flight.
Every chord a story told,
In tender verses, love unfolds.

The rhythm drives our restless hearts,
In this song, a spark that starts.
In every pause, we hold our breath,
Feeling life, and flirting with death.

So we strum the strings of fate,
In melodies we resonate.
Together in this sweet embrace,
Through music, we find our place.

Dance of Zeal

In the heart beats a rhythm,
Feet move with fervent grace,
Spinning dreams on the floor,
Lost in passion's embrace.

Every glance, a silent spark,
Echoes in the night air,
Waves of joy, we embark,
Unveiling magic to share.

The music calls, we respond,
Fingers brush in twilight's glow,
With each step, we are fond,
In this moment, time slows.

Bright eyes shine like the stars,
A dance born from our fire,
Together we've come so far,
Fueled by our deep desire.

Both rhythm and heart entwined,
As shadows softly sway,
In this dance, love defined,
Here forever, we'll stay.

Unyielding Fire

In the depths, a flame ignites,
Pushing through the night, bold,
Bearing witness to the fights,
Stories of the brave unfold.

Rising fierce like the dawn,
Hearts ablaze with strong intent,
In the ashes, hope is drawn,
Reflections of the time spent.

Through the storms, we will stand,
With a spark that won't die down,
Together, hand in hand,
A testament in this town.

Our laughter is the fuel,
Turning shadows into light,
With each heartbeat, we rule,
An unyielding, blazing sight.

In the embers of our fight,
The warmth of love remains,
Forever holding on tight,
We will break all the chains.

Serenade of Secrets

Underneath the silver moon,
Whispers dance on the breeze,
Every note a sweet tune,
Hidden hearts find some ease.

In the garden of our dreams,
Soft petals kiss the night air,
Flickering light gently beams,
As we share secrets rare.

With each sigh, a story blooms,
Wrapped in shadows and time,
Casting spells, erasing gloom,
Together, we create rhyme.

Eyes like stars, so profound,
Hold the mysteries untold,
In silence, love can be found,
A serenade to behold.

In this realm of soft sighs,
Every heartbeat, a soft plea,
Amongst the stars, love flies,
Whispered futures, you and me.

Infatuation's Echo

A glance from you sends me reeling,
Thoughts swirl like the autumn leaves,
Caught in this sweet revealing,
Time halts as my heart believes.

In a room, the world fades out,
Echoes of laughter ignite,
With you, there's never a doubt,
Every moment feels so right.

The pulse of young hearts so bold,
Every shared breath a delight,
In your eyes, stories unfold,
Dreaming deep into the night.

Like whispers that brush the skin,
Infatuation's gentle song,
Tangled thoughts like a win,
In this feeling, we belong.

As the stars align above,
Let's capture this fleeting bliss,
Every heartbeat speaks of love,
In your gaze, I find my kiss.

Vibrant Embrace

In the garden where colors bloom,
We dance together, chasing the gloom.
Whispers of joy fill the air,
In every heartbeat, love's sweet care.

Underneath a sky of blue,
We find the warmth in every hue.
Hands entwined, we share this grace,
Lost in the magic of our embrace.

Each petal falls, a story told,
In laughter and dreams, we dare be bold.
Time stands still in this wondrous space,
Wrapped in love's gentle embrace.

Through the night, the stars will gleam,
Guiding us softly, like a dream.
With every sigh, our spirits soar,
In vibrant love, forevermore.

So let us dance beneath the light,
In the embrace of endless night.
With every heartbeat, we thrive and race,
Together always, a vibrant embrace.

Luminous Devotion

In quiet corners, secrets flow,
A light that through our hearts will glow.
Beneath the moon, our spirits rise,
In luminous waves, love never dies.

Each promise made with gentle grace,
A tapestry we weave, embrace.
Through trials faced, hand in hand,
In devotion's warmth, we proudly stand.

With every dawn that paints the skies,
A new beginning, love never lies.
In the whispers of the morning sun,
Our journey blooms, forever one.

As shadows stretch and daylight fades,
Our hearts aflame, the music played.
In every chord, a sweet emotion,
Bound forever in this devotion.

So let us walk through fields of gold,
Hand in hand, let our stories unfold.
In every heartbeat, life we'll own,
In luminous love, we're never alone.

Melodies of Love

In the quiet of a gentle night,
Soft serenades take joyful flight.
Each note a whisper, sweetly spun,
In the melodies of love, we're one.

Through the storms and skies of gray,
Your voice continues to light the way.
In rhythm and rhyme, our hearts align,
In every heartbeat, your love is mine.

The symphony of dreams unfolds,
With every tale, our love retold.
Through echoes of laughter and tears,
Melodies linger throughout the years.

As stars ignite in the velvet night,
Every glance, a spark, a light.
With you, the world finds its song,
In harmony where we belong.

So let the music play and swell,
A tale of love we know so well.
In the dance of time, let passion steer,
In melodies of love, forever near.

Heartstrings and Harmonies

With every strum of love's sweet tune,
Hearts collide beneath the moon.
In whispered words that gently sway,
Our heartstrings bind, come what may.

In the echoes of laughter's call,
Together we rise, together we fall.
Each harmony weaves a tender thread,
In the tapestry of love, we're led.

As seasons change and moments flee,
Our symphony sings eternally.
With every heartbeat, a song refined,
In perfect rhythm, our souls aligned.

Through the trials and the storms we face,
In every challenge, we find our place.
Intertwined in the sweetest sound,
In heartstrings and harmonies, love is found.

So let us dance to this sacred song,
In joy and pain, we both belong.
Together forever, a timeless refrain,
In heartstrings and harmonies, always remain.

Serendipity's Gaze

In whispers soft, fate intertwines,
Unexpected paths where joy aligns.
A fleeting glance, a chance encounter,
Magic blooms like spring's sweet counter.

Threads of laughter weave through the day,
Guiding hearts in a gentle sway.
Moments unfurl, like petals in light,
Serendipity dances in the night.

Paths once crossed now embrace the new,
In every moment, colors accrue.
Life's hidden treasures, found in surprise,
Each step a journey, a wondrous rise.

A glance exchanged, the world feels bright,
In the simplicity, pure delight.
Time stands still, in radiant embrace,
With serendipity's gaze, we find our place.

Seasons change, yet the heart stays true,
In the tapestry, me and you.
A bond unspoken, yet deeply known,
In every smile, our love has grown.

Flame of Inspiration

In the stillness, a spark ignites,
Whispers of dreams on starry nights.
Ideas take flight like birds in the air,
Guided by passion, beyond compare.

A flicker begins, consuming the dark,
Setting ablaze every hidden spark.
Creativity flows like a river wide,
With the flame of inspiration as our guide.

In the quiet moments, it screams bold,
A story untold, waiting to unfold.
Colors collide, bright canvases tease,
With every brushstroke, our spirits seize.

Chasing the shadows, we dance in the light,
Illumined by hopes, our hearts feel light.
The flame flickers on, never to tire,
In the depths of our soul, lives the fire.

From ashes we rise, the phoenix flies high,
Bound by the dreams we dare to deny.
Flame of inspiration, forever will glow,
In the heart of the artist, starlit and aglow.

Tethered Souls

In the quiet, our hearts align,
Tethered souls in love divine.
Across the stars, we hear the call,
Together we rise, or together we fall.

Threads invisible, yet strong and true,
In this vast world, it's me and you.
Through trials and joys, we weave our story,
Tethered souls bask in love's true glory.

In laughter shared, in tears we find,
A bond unbreakable, forever entwined.
Together we soar, on winds of grace,
In each other's arms, we've found our place.

Every heartbeat whispers your name,
In this dance of life, it's never the same.
Journeying forward, come what may,
Tethered souls light the darkest day.

With every moment, our spirits ignite,
Guided together, through day and night.
In the tapestry of time, love entwines,
Tethered souls, where destiny shines.

Inner Fire

Deep within, a flame resides,
An inner fire that never hides.
Through shadows thick, it fiercely glows,
Guiding the path, where courage flows.

In moments of doubt, it rages bright,
A beacon of hope in the heart of the night.
With every challenge, it sparks anew,
Fueling the dreams that we dare pursue.

Whispers of passion, a relentless chase,
In the quiet moments, we find our place.
The embers of purpose, steadily rise,
In the depths of our soul, a warrior cries.

Through storms and trials, we stand tall,
With inner fire, we'll conquer all.
In the tapestry woven, our spirits rise,
Igniting the world with fervent skies.

The journey unfolds, a courageous song,
In the heart's embrace, we all belong.
Inner fire burns, a relentless aspire,
In the essence of life, we'll forever inspire.

Fires of the Heart

In the quiet glow of twilight's gleam,
Embers dance, igniting dreams.
Whispers linger in the air,
Passions flame with tender care.

With every spark that dares to rise,
Hope ignites beneath the skies.
Hearts entwined like vines that coil,
In this heat, their love will toil.

Through shadows long and nights so still,
They chase the warmth, they feel the thrill.
Fires smolder, deep and bright,
Guiding souls through the night.

In the blaze, their fears dissolve,
In the flames, each heart evolves.
Together they forge a path anew,
Bound by love, forever true.

Whispers of Desire

Beneath the stars, soft voices sigh,
Desire whispers, never shy.
In secret glances, longing grows,
A dance of heartbeats, passion flows.

As moonlight drapes the world in silk,
Words exchanged like breath and milk.
Each touch ignites a spark divine,
In the quiet, their souls entwine.

Through tangled sheets and echoes sweet,
Time slips by, a stolen beat.
Promises linger in the dark,
A gentle flame, a hidden spark.

In the silence, they find their voice,
In the moment, hearts rejoice.
With whispered hopes that brave the night,
They chase the dawn, their shared delight.

Flames Beneath the Surface

Deep within, where shadows dwell,
Flames flicker, casting spells.
Beneath the calm, a tempest stirs,
Yearning whispers prompt their purrs.

Like molten gold, their feelings flow,
In hidden depths, they come to know.
Love's heat lies dormant, waiting there,
In silent hopes and secret prayer.

Through trials faced and battles fought,
The fire rages, lessons taught.
In quiet moments, kindred souls
Ignite the spark that makes them whole.

Surrounded by a world so cold,
Their connection, a tale untold.
With each heartbeat, the flames arise,
Fueling passion that never dies.

Unchained Hearts

In freedom's embrace, love takes flight,
Two hearts unchained, igniting the night.
No chains can bind what souls ignite,
Together they soar, hearts alight.

With laughter shared in open fields,
They uncover the beauty that love wields.
In every glance, a promise blooms,
Dancing away each shadowed gloom.

Through valleys low and mountains high,
With hands entwined, they reach the sky.
Every step taken, a sacred vow,
In this moment, they live for now.

Their journey unfolds, a tapestry bright,
Painting their days with joy and light.
In the symphony of shared embrace,
Unchained hearts find their place.

Thorns and Petals

In a garden lush and bright,
Thorns guard petals glowing light.
Beauty dances in the breeze,
Yet hidden pain brings us to knees.

Softly whispers secrets old,
Stories of the brave and bold.
Each thorn a trial, each petal grace,
Together they form a tender space.

Love and heartache intertwined,
In this sacred bond, we find.
The beauty in our scars displayed,
In every memory, unafraid.

Hold the thorns, embrace the pain,
From the storm, new blooms remain.
In the struggle, strength revealed,
Thorns and petals, wounds healed.

Every blossom tells a tale,
Of resilience when we fail.
In the cycle of joy and grief,
Thorns and petals offer relief.

Tempest of Tenderness

Winds howl with a fierce embrace,
Yet tenderness finds its place.
Storms may rage and shadows fall,
In the chaos, love stands tall.

Lightning strikes, a flash of heat,
Soft whispers warm the cold defeat.
In the heart of tempest's night,
Gentle souls take flight with light.

Raindrops dance upon the ground,
In every drop, a heart is found.
Through the turmoil, hope takes form,
A shelter from the raging storm.

Amidst the thunder, peace we seek,
With every clash, the strong, the meek.
Tempest wild, yet kindness flows,
In depth of chaos, love still grows.

From the ashes, blooms appear,
In the storm, we conquer fear.
Tender hearts, fierce and brave,
In a tempest, love we save.

Ignited Spirits

Flickers glow in darkest night,
Holding strength, igniting light.
In the depths of shadows cast,
Our spirits rise, no fear amassed.

Embers dance with souls aflame,
In unity, we stake our claim.
Voices echo, courage sworn,
From ashes, new hopes are born.

In a world of endless doubt,
We find the fire, voices shout.
Together, we can forge a path,
Unyielding joy, we face the wrath.

Each heartbeat fuels the flame,
Our spirits wild, never tame.
Together, we weave our song,
With ignited spirits, we belong.

Radiant sparks against the night,
In our hearts, we find the light.
With every step, we rise anew,
Ignited spirits, strong and true.

In the Depths of Yearning

Whispers echo through the night,
In the depths, we seek the light.
A longing heart, a silent plea,
In shadows deep, we yearn to be.

The stars above, a distant dream,
In our hearts, a hopeful gleam.
Searching souls for paths unknown,
In the depths, we find our own.

Every tear holds a story spun,
In the yearning, battles won.
Through the sorrow, strength remains,
In this dance of aches and gains.

Love like rivers, fierce and free,
In each moment, we believe.
In yearning's depth, we find our song,
A melody where we belong.

Though time may stretch, our hearts ignite,
In the depths, together, we fight.
Bound by dreams, forever tethered,
In yearning's embrace, we are weathered.

Surrender to the Heart

In shadows deep where choices lie,
A whisper calls, a soft goodbye.
The heart, it tugs with gentle grace,
In surrender's warmth, we find our place.

Let go of fears that bind the soul,
Embrace the truth that makes us whole.
With open arms, we dare to feel,
In the still night, our wounds can heal.

Through storms that rage and winds that howl,
We dance to rhythms, the heart's sweet vowel.
Together we rise, unbroken, free,
In love's embrace, we find our key.

The world may pull in harsh dismay,
But softness shines, it lights our way.
In every beat, our spirits sing,
Surrender sweet, to what love brings.

Unraveled Emotions

Threads of feeling, tangled tight,
In the quiet, we seek the light.
Each moment whispers, soft and slow,
Unraveled tales, the heart will know.

Joy and sorrow, hand in hand,
We weave our lives, like grains of sand.
With every tear, a glimpse of truth,
In vibrant hues, we embrace our youth.

The depth of pain, a soul's release,
In shattered dreams, we find our peace.
Through tender moments, laughter's grace,
Emotions speak in this sacred space.

As seasons change, so do we grow,
In shades of love, in ebb and flow.
Through storms and stillness, we will learn,
Unraveled hearts will always yearn.

Chasing Starlit Hopes

Beneath the night, the stars align,
We chase our dreams, a world divine.
With every twinkle, hopes arise,
In endless skies, our spirit flies.

The journey long, the path unclear,
But starlit whispers draw us near.
With every step, the dark shall fade,
In twilight's glow, our fears displayed.

Through valleys deep, on mountains high,
We'll seek the wonders in the sky.
With open hearts, we'll find our way,
Chasing the dawn of a brand new day.

In shadows cast by dreams anew,
We gather strength from skies so blue.
Together we rise, hand in hand,
Chasing starlit hopes across the land.

Nectar of the Soul

In quiet moments, sweetness brews,
A nectar rich, a soulful muse.
Each drop a blessing, soft and pure,
In love's embrace, our spirits cure.

The garden blooms with fragrant grace,
In every heartbeat, we find our place.
With laughter's echo, we drink it in,
The nectar flows, where love begins.

Through trials faced, we take a sip,
In bitter times, let kindness grip.
With open hearts, we share the gold,
The stories passed, forever told.

In dance of life, we twirl and spin,
In every loss, new growth begins.
The nectar calls, sweet and deep,
In every joy, our souls shall leap.

Cherished Spark

In the quiet of the night,
A flicker softly glows,
Hearts align and take flight,
Where true affection flows.

Memories dance like fireflies,
Whispers wrap in embrace,
Moments held beneath the skies,
A timeless, cherished place.

In laughter shared, joy ignites,
Each glance a tender thread,
Guiding through the darkest nights,
Where love is gently spread.

With every heartbeat, we weave,
A tapestry divine,
In dreams, we're free to believe,
Together, you and I.

A spark that shines ever bright,
Eternal and sincere,
In the depths of endless night,
Your presence, always near.

Portraits of Euphoria

Brush strokes of vibrant hues,
Canvas alive with delight,
Moments to forever choose,
In the day and through the night.

Laughter painted in the air,
Colors swirling with great zeal,
Every heartbeat laid bare,
Showcasing how we feel.

Through the windows of our soul,
Reflections cast in light,
In every dream, we make whole,
A glimpse of pure delight.

Such beauty in our embrace,
Where time slows to a crawl,
In this fleeting, sacred space,
We rise and never fall.

Life's gallery we roam free,
Each portrait tells a tale,
In the joy of you and me,
Our love will never pale.

Symmetry of Emotions

In the dance of heartbeats true,
Two souls entwined in grace,
Reflecting every hue,
In this sacred space.

Tides of joy and waves of pain,
Balance in the flow,
Through the sunshine and the rain,
Together, we shall grow.

In the echoes of our past,
We find our way anew,
In the shadows, light is cast,
Rendering hope with you.

Every glance a steadfast guide,
In this vast array,
With you, there's nothing left to hide,
Our hearts will find a way.

In the symmetry, we stand strong,
United, firm, and free,
In this melody, our song,
A beautiful decree.

Fragmented Dreams

Scattered pieces float in air,
Whispers of what should have been,
In the silence, secrets bare,
Weaves a tale, hard and keen.

Moments lost in tangled threads,
Chasing shadows of despair,
Where the silence softly spreads,
Longing for the love we share.

Fleeting thoughts like silken smoke,
Drifting through the night,
In the shards, we find a cloak,
Wrapping dreams in light.

Every heartbeat, fragmented sighs,
Piecing hope from the gloom,
Beneath the vast and starry skies,
Resurrecting every bloom.

In the cracks, we still will find,
A path to carry on,
With each heartbeat intertwined,
Our dreams will not be gone.

Zones of Tenderness

In quiet corners, love resides,
Soft whispers linger, hearts collide.
Gentle touches, a warm embrace,
In these zones, we find our place.

With every glance, a spark ignites,
A dance of shadows, moonlit nights.
In tenderness, our fears unwind,
A haven found, two souls aligned.

We wander through the fields of grace,
Where softness blooms, a sacred space.
In blooming flowers, secrets grow,
In zones of tenderness, love flows.

Each heartbeat whispers, soft and shy,
In twilight moments, we can't deny.
Connections woven strong and true,
In these zones, it's me and you.

Together here, we break the mold,
In simple gestures, stories told.
With every sigh, our worries fade,
In these zones, our love conveyed.

Unhinged Souls

In the chaos, we find our tune,
Dancing swiftly, under the moon.
Unhinged moments, wild and free,
A symphony of you and me.

Through broken fences, dreams unbound,
In the madness, our truth is found.
Fractured pieces gleam and shine,
Unhinged souls, forever entwined.

Electric sparks in every glance,
A reckless wave, a daring chance.
In stormy tides, we sail away,
Unhinged souls, come what may.

With hearts ablaze, we chase the night,
Finding solace in our fight.
Together, we embrace the scar,
In this madness, we raise the bar.

Through every tear and every laugh,
We carve a path, our perfect cleft.
Unchained spirits, wild and bold,
In our chaos, we break the mold.

Destined Hearts

Under starlit skies, we roam,
Two destined hearts, we found our home.
Threads of fate, they intertwine,
A love story that's yours and mine.

In fleeting moments, time stands still,
With every heartbeat, an unspoken thrill.
In shadow's dance, our futures blend,
On this journey, love shall transcend.

With every breath, a whisper shared,
In perfect harmony, we dared.
The universe sings in vibrant hues,
Destined hearts, we cannot lose.

In quiet mornings, hand in hand,
Together we venture, bold and grand.
Each step we take, a story unfolds,
In this tapestry, our love beholds.

Through storms we soar, through light we shine,
With every challenge, our hearts realign.
Destined souls, forever true,
In this life, I choose you.

Veil of Attraction

Behind the veil, mysteries hide,
An attraction deeper than the tide.
In glances swift, our truths are bare,
A silent pull, a magnetic flare.

With every laugh, our spirits rise,
In a world where passion defies.
The veil lifts slowly, inch by inch,
In painted moments, never a clinch.

We navigate this dance of fate,
Entangled fates, we celebrate.
In shadows cast by candlelight,
Veil of attraction, pure delight.

With whispered dreams upon our lips,
We take the plunge, embrace the risks.
Through every storm, our hearts align,
In the veil, our souls entwine.

Step by step, we break the chain,
A bond unyielding, free from pain.
Underneath the stars, we find,
Veil of attraction, hearts combined.

Embrace of Recklessness

In twilight's glow, we dance with fate,
Chasing shadows we can hardly rate,
Whispers of thrill beckon our hearts,
Pushing limits, where freedom starts.

With every step, the danger sings,
A melody of uncharted things,
Fear and joy, a twisted blend,
In this moment, we transcend.

The world is vast, its edges blurred,
We dive into the wild, unheard,
Laughing loud, our spirits soar,
Embrace the reckless, crave for more.

Hold my hand, let chaos reign,
Together we'll dance through pleasure and pain,
In every heartbeat, a promise lies,
The thrill of life fills our skies.

So let us linger, on this edge so bright,
Even in darkness, we find our light,
Within the pulse of our reckless plight,
We learn to live, to love, to fight.

Passion's Palette

With strokes of fire, our spirits collide,
Colors of longing we cannot hide,
Every hue a secret desire,
In the canvas of hearts, we conspire.

Crimson dreams and sapphire tears,
We paint our canvas, facing fears,
Brushes dancing in playful delight,
Creating worlds within the night.

From gentle whispers to bold displays,
Our love ignites in myriad ways,
On this palette, emotions flow,
A masterpiece no one can know.

Vivid moments blend and swirl,
In passion's tide, we find our world,
With every stroke, we claim the day,
In this art of love, we forever stay.

So let's create, just you and I,
A universe where colors fly,
In every shade, our souls entwine,
Together, love, we'll always shine.

Resonance of Life

In quiet moments, echoes play,
A symphony of night and day,
Each heartbeat sings a vivid tone,
A whispered truth we've always known.

Through storms and calm, the rhythm sways,
Life's melody in endless praise,
From laughter's song to sorrow's breath,
Each note weaves tales of life and death.

With open hearts, we find the way,
In every life, a debt to pay,
The chords of love, the strings of time,
In harmony, we seek the climb.

Like waves that crash on golden sands,
Together we traverse this land,
With hands held tight, we face the strife,
In the resonance, we find our life.

So sing with me, let voices rise,
In unity, beneath vast skies,
For in this chorus, we belong,
The resonance of life, our song.

Labyrinth of Desire

In winding paths, our fantasies dwell,
A maze of longing where secrets swell,
Each turn reveals a new surprise,
In the labyrinth of our desires.

With shadows lurking, whispers tease,
Lost in reverie, we find our ease,
The walls resonate with silent screams,
Each echo leads to hidden dreams.

Through twisting alleys of lust and light,
We chase the thrill, both day and night,
With every breath, the tension grows,
In this puzzle, our passion flows.

Beyond the corners, the heartbeats race,
In this intricate, enchanting space,
We wander freely, no end in sight,
Lost in the depths of desire's bite.

So take my hand, let's lose control,
In this labyrinth, we find our soul,
For in the maze, we learn to play,
Embracing desire, come what may.

A Symphony of Embers

Flickers dance in twilight's embrace,
Whispers echo in the soft space.
The night holds secrets, warm and bright,
Each ember glows, a fleeting light.

Dancing shadows play on the ground,
In their rhythm, a silence found.
Crackling fire sings its song,
In the dark, where hearts belong.

An orchestra of crackling flame,
In every spark, we feel the same.
Memories rise like smoke in air,
Captured moments, beyond compare.

Underneath the starry shroud,
Nature sways, gentle and proud.
Embers flicker, stories unfurl,
In the night, a magical whirl.

The symphony of night ignites,
With every twinkle, pure delights.
In this dance, we find a way,
To lose ourselves, to light the day.

Captivated by You

In your gaze, the world stands still,
Ocean depths, an endless thrill.
Every heartbeat sings a tune,
Underneath the silver moon.

Moments captured, time suspended,
With each glance, our dreams extended.
Whispers soft as evening's sigh,
In your arms, I learn to fly.

Magic weaves through every touch,
In this dance, I feel so much.
Every laugh, a gentle breeze,
Lost in you, I find my ease.

The stars align when you are near,
Time dissolves, and all is clear.
With every breath, we intertwine,
In this space, forever mine.

Captivated, hearts ablaze,
In your light, I'll forever gaze.
In this love, we'll always stay,
Guided by the dawn of day.

Nightfall's Caress

A velvet cloak descends at dusk,
In shadows deep, there's a husk.
Softly whispers of the night,
Cradling dreams in twinkling light.

The moon, a watchful, silver eye,
Paints the world as night drifts by.
Stars awaken, one by one,
Embraced within the darkened fun.

Cool breezes weave a gentle song,
Undulating, where we belong.
In the hush, a lullaby,
Carried forth through winds that sigh.

Every heartbeat, syncopated,
In the stillness, hearts elated.
Nightfall's touch, a soothing balm,
In chaos, find a perfect calm.

As twilight dances with the breeze,
Wrapped in dreams beneath the trees.
Nightfall's caress, pure and true,
In this moment, lost in you.

The Art of Surrender

In the stillness, let it go,
Breathe in deep; feel the flow.
Every fear, like leaves, will fall,
Surrendering to nature's call.

Waves of time wash over me,
In the current, I am free.
Letting go of what I know,
In this space, I learn to grow.

Every heartbeat, pure and wild,
Finds the essence of the child.
Trust the journey, cast the line,
In the depths, your spirit shines.

Like a flower breaking through,
Embrace the light, let it ring true.
In the dance of give and take,
Feel the world as dreams awake.

The art of surrender feels divine,
In chaos, find a heart that shines.
With open arms, I welcome peace,
In this moment, I find release.

Breathless Yearnings

In the hush of night, dreams take flight,
Whispers of wishes nestled tight.
Hearts race with hopes yet untold,
In the silence, passions unfold.

Fingers trace the cool, soft air,
Yearning glances caught in despair.
Moments linger, sweet and shy,
Breathless wishes soaring high.

Every heartbeat sings your name,
In the depths, a roaring flame.
Time stands still as shadows play,
Chasing echoes of the day.

Lost in thoughts and visions bright,
Chasing dreams under starlit night.
With every breath, the world fades,
In this dance, our love cascades.

Yet the dawn will bring its light,
Colors bleed, illusions fight.
But in shadows, we reside,
Wrapped in love, forever tied.

Echoes of Longing

In the silence, whispers creep,
Memories of moments we keep.
A melody rings through the air,
Echoes of love, subtle and rare.

Through the layers of night's embrace,
I feel the warmth of your trace.
Every heartbeat a knowing glance,
Two souls lost in a timeless dance.

Time may change the path we tread,
But love's essence can't be shed.
With each sigh, the past unfolds,
In echoes of stories retold.

Cascading dreams like silver streams,
Filling the void with gentle beams.
In the quiet, we're intertwined,
Together within the heart's mind.

While life speeds on, we stand still,
Moments etched, the heart can fill.
In every echo, I find you,
A love enduring, always true.

Tides of Affection

Gentle waves caress the shore,
Each rise and fall, love's sweet score.
Tides of passion, ebb and flow,
In this dance, our feelings grow.

With every whisper, the sea sighs,
Underneath the sprawling skies.
Footprints left in golden sand,
Memories shared, hand in hand.

Stars above watch our embrace,
Guiding hearts through time and space.
Every heartbeat, a soft refrain,
Together we weather the rain.

The moon it pulls with gentle might,
Stirring souls in the still night.
As seas collide and merge as one,
In luminous glow, our love begun.

When the tide retreats, do not fear,
For in my heart, you'll always be near.
In the depths of our affection's sway,
Love, like the sea, will always stay.

When Stars Collide

In a cosmos vast and deep,
Where shadows play and secrets sleep.
Two hearts meet, a fateful spark,
Illuminating worlds so dark.

Stars aligned in silent grace,
And in that moment, time did race.
Galaxies spun with every sigh,
Creating constellations high.

With every glance, sparks ignite,
Guided by the soft moonlight.
A universe that feels so right,
When love blooms in the dead of night.

Through cosmic dust, we find our way,
Waltzing lightly, come what may.
In the dance of time and fate,
We find the love that won't abate.

When stars collide and hearts entwine,
Infinite threads of fate align.
In this vastness, I call you home,
In your heart, I'll always roam.

Clandestine Kisses

In the shadows where whispers dwell,
Two hearts conspire, secrets to tell.
Soft touches stolen in the night,
Wrapped in silence, hearts take flight.

Under the moon's watchful eye,
Promises spoken, none can deny.
A dance of lips, a fleeting chance,
In hidden corners, the lovers prance.

Time stands still, a fleeting embrace,
As starlit dreams illuminate space.
The world outside fades to a blur,
While in this moment, passions stir.

Glistening souls, a pact unknown,
Clandestine kisses in twilight's throne.
With every glance, a world apart,
Unity forged within each heart.

Yet day will dawn, and shadows flee,
But in the dim, they'll always be.
Bound by the night, the warmth persists,
In every memory, love exists.

Lighthouses of Longing

On distant shores, where waves crash loud,
Lighthouses stand, sturdy and proud.
Guiding the lost with beams of light,
Through darkest hours, they spark the night.

Across the seas where dreams take flight,
A beacon calls, igniting the night.
With each pulse, hope flickers bright,
Yearning hearts drawn to its sight.

In storms of doubt, they glow fierce and true,
A signal heard by a soul or two.
Distance may wane, but wishes survive,
In the lighthouse glow, love will thrive.

Bound by the waves, our spirits entwined,
Across the water, our fates aligned.
In every splash, in every sigh,
Lighthouses stand where secrets lie.

When dawn breaks over the tempest's shelf,
We will find our way, rediscover ourselves.
In each rising tide, longing speaks loud,
Lighthouses of longing, eternally proud.

Invincible Bonds

Through storms that rage and winds that howl,
Together we stand, a resolute vow.
In the face of trials, our spirits unite,
Forging invincible bonds in the night.

With laughter shared and silent tears,
We weave a tapestry, calming fears.
Hands held tight, through thick and thin,
A testament of love, where hope begins.

Time may test, but we shall endure,
Stronger together, our hearts remain pure.
In every heartbeat, a story is spun,
Invincible bonds, two lives as one.

Through the darkest valleys, we will roam,
In the arms of each other, always home.
Infinite trust, like stars in the night,
Guides us forever, our spirits alight.

When shadows fall and daylight fades,
In our embrace, no fear invades.
For in this journey, love's truth confounds,
Wrapped in the warmth of invincible bounds.

Whirlwind of Emotion

Caught in the storm of a fierce embrace,
A whirlwind of feelings, we lose our place.
Every glance ignites the air,
In this tempest, nothing can compare.

Spinning like leaves in autumn's dance,
Our hearts entwined in a blissful trance.
Every heartbeat echoes loud,
In this chaos, we stand proud.

Joy and sorrow, a delicate blend,
In the eye of the storm, love will mend.
Passions collide like thunder and rain,
In this whirlwind, there's no room for pain.

With every turn, new colors appear,
Brilliant shades of hope, courage, and fear.
The tempest roars, yet we find calm,
In the storm's eye, we are the balm.

When the winds settle and silence reigns,
We'll cherish the storms, embrace the pains.
In the quiet aftermath, love's roots grow,
In this whirlwind, endlessly aglow.

Heartbeats in Harmony

One heartbeat whispers, slow and sure,
In the dance of shadows, love endures.
Each pulse a rhythm, soft and bright,
Together we glow in the gentle night.

When eyes meet softly, silence speaks,
A language of longing, where courage peaks.
Two souls entwined, a perfect blend,
In the warmth of dusk, our hearts extend.

Every sigh echoes, a sweet refrain,
In the tapestry woven, love's no strain.
Harmony lingers, a soft embrace,
In a world united, we find our place.

With every beat, the universe sways,
Together we bask in the sun's warm rays.
With heartbeats in sync, our spirits fly,
In the embrace of love, we'll always try.

So let the world whisper its gentle song,
With you beside me, I know I belong.
In the symphony of life, we create,
Heartbeats in harmony, our wondrous fate.

Intimate Currents

Tender breezes intertwine and flow,
In the quiet moments, feelings grow.
Each glance a spark, igniting the flame,
Intimate currents, always the same.

As shadows merge, we stray from the light,
Wrapped in whispers that dance through the night.
Our hearts beat softly, in synchrony true,
In the silence of us, a world anew.

Every heartbeat mirrors, every sigh shares,
Hidden connections flow, no one cares.
In the depths of dreaming, we softly glide,
Intimate currents, where love won't hide.

The moonlight spills secrets, softly aglow,
In every moment where time feels slow.
As waves crash gently, our spirits dive,
In the ocean of trust, we feel alive.

With fingers entwined, we navigate fate,
In currents uncharted, we celebrate.
Love wrapped in silence, a soothing art,
Intimate currents, the pulse of the heart.

A Surrendered Heart

In the echoes of longing, I find my way,
A surrendered heart, willing to stay.
With every heartbeat, a promise made,
In love's embrace, all fears will fade.

Each whispered secret, a gentle bond,
From shadows of doubt, we craft beyond.
Leaving behind what once held tight,
Together, we leap into the light.

With open arms, I let you in,
In the warmth of your gaze, my journey begins.
The walls I built start to dissolve,
In the magic of trust, our spirits evolve.

With love's sweet embrace, I breathe you near,
A tapestry woven, no room for fear.
In the stillness, we find our peace,
A surrendered heart, where love won't cease.

Hand in hand, through storms we'll glide,
In the dance of the years, forever side by side.
With courage to love, we will not part,
In every beat, a surrendered heart.

Echoes of Enthusiasm

In the dawn's first light, hope stirs awake,
With every laugh, new paths we stake.
The world a canvas, bright and wide,
In echoes of enthusiasm, hearts abide.

As whispers of joy rise with the sun,
In the rhythm of life, we are one.
Each moment radiant, vibrant and clear,
In echoes of laughter, we conquer fear.

Every challenge met with open arms,
In the dance of life, we find our charms.
With every heartbeat, possibilities grow,
In the spirit of daring, we live the flow.

From sunlit hills to the ocean's swell,
In every adventure, our stories tell.
With hearts unguarded, we chase the stars,
In echoes of enthusiasm, no more scars.

Together we march, fueled by our dreams,
In the wisdom of love, nothing is as it seems.
With each step forward, we'll never depart,
In echoes of enthusiasm, we ignite the heart.

Whispers in the Dark

In shadows deep, secrets creep,
Silent echoes, dreams to keep.
Moonlight dances on quiet sighs,
Whispers linger, the heart complies.

Underneath the velvet night,
Stars confide in silver light.
Faintest murmur, soft and low,
Guiding souls where few can go.

A breathless hush fills the air,
Promises linger, light as prayer.
Lost in thoughts, drifting afar,
Embracing freedom, a shooting star.

Moments shared, a tender thread,
Words unspoken, hearts are fed.
In this realm, we find our way,
Whispers echo, night to day.

Together bound, yet far apart,
In the silence, beats a heart.
Softly weaving dreams anew,
In the dark, I still find you.

Threads of Euphoria

Threads of gold in twilight glow,
Woven dreams begin to flow.
With every heartbeat, hope ascends,
In a dance where joy extends.

Colors swirl in dizzy flight,
Laughter sparkles, pure delight.
Moments twine, a tapestry,
Crafting bliss in unity.

Through the chaos, light we find,
Every heartbeat, intertwined.
Joyful echoes fill the air,
Euphoria, beyond compare.

Hands entwined, we chase the sun,
In this journey, we are one.
Every step, a melody,
Threads of love, eternity.

Seasons change, yet still we rise,
In each other, we find skies.
Threading dreams in colors bright,
We are euphoria's pure light.

The Pulse of Connection

In the silence, hearts align,
Rhythms echo, yours and mine.
A gentle thrum in the stillness,
Connection forms in pure wellness.

Eyes meet softly, souls awake,
In this moment, choices make.
Shared laughter, whispers collide,
A pulse ignites, worlds opened wide.

With every beat, a story told,
In this dance, we brave and bold.
Fragments of life intertwine,
Creating bonds that brightly shine.

Distance fades, love draws us near,
In the pulse, we lose all fear.
With every breath, we start anew,
Our hearts speak words unspoken too.

With time's flow, we stand as one,
Connection felt, never undone.
In the rhythm, life we treasure,
The pulse of love, our greatest measure.

A Symphony of Hearts

In the stillness, music calls,
A symphony within us thralls.
Notes of laughter, strains of pain,
In harmony, we rise again.

With each heartbeat, chords align,
Melodies sweet, purely divine.
Strings of love, they gently play,
Guiding us, come what may.

Echoes of dreams in chorus sing,
Through the storm, together we bring.
In the dance of dusk till dawn,
A symphony that carries on.

In the twilight, rhythms blend,
Every note a heart to mend.
Together we create a song,
In this journey, we belong.

As the final curtain falls,
Resilient love within us calls.
In this symphony, forever we'll stay,
Hearts entwined, come what may.

Infatuation's Journey

In the hush of night, hearts begin to soar,
Eyes like stars, forever wanting more.
A glimmer of hope, whispering it seems,
Taking a step into tangled dreams.

Every glance exchanged, a spark ignites,
Lost in the magic of fleeting lights.
Moments hanging like dew on a rose,
In this sweet madness, the wildness grows.

With each fleeting touch, a story unfolds,
Secrets entwined in the silence it holds.
Caught in the rush of the heart's wild beat,
In the warmth of desire, two souls meet.

At the edge of doubt, we take a chance,
Caught in the rhythm of a daring dance.
With laughter and whispers, we learn the art,
Of weaving our lives, two souls, one heart.

As the dawn approaches, we hold our breath,
A journey begun, not bound by regret.
With each step we take, we forge our own way,
In infatuation's glow, forever we'll stay.

Threads of Devotion

In the quiet space where love aligns,
We weave together our hearts like vines.
Each thread a promise, strong and true,
Intertwined stories of me and you.

With every sunrise, new colors appear,
A tapestry growing, stitched with cheer.
Through trials and joys, we hold it tight,
Guided by stars that shine in the night.

Your laughter a song that echoes my soul,
In the fabric of time, we merge and console.
Woven in trust, with stitches of grace,
Each moment a bead, in time's gentle pace.

With gentle whispers, we map out our dreams,
Sailing on hopes, like sunlit streams.
Bound by affection, through trials we stand,
Together, forever, hand in hand.

As the seasons shift, our colors remain,
In the warmth of devotion, there's nothing but gain.
With every heartbeat, our story will grow,
Threads of devotion, a radiant glow.

Shadows of Enchantment

In the dim-lit glow, where secrets reside,
Shadows dance lightly, as dreams coincide.
A flicker of starlight, a heartbeat away,
In the realm of enchantment, together we sway.

Whispers of magic in a soft, tender breeze,
Moments suspended, our hearts at ease.
Lost in the twilight, where dreams softly call,
We fade into shadows, enchanted by it all.

Every glance shared, a silent embrace,
In the twilight's glow, we find our place.
With laughter like music, sweet and sincere,
In the shadowy haze, it's only you near.

As the night unfolds, we linger and hide,
Dancing through visions, lost in the tide.
With every heartbeat, a spell we compose,
In shadows of enchantment, love only grows.

When dawn breaks gentle and pulls us from dreams,
We carry the magic, or so it seems.
A world painted vibrant, with hues so bold,
In the shadows we journey, our story retold.

Colors of Unspoken Feelings

In quiet glances, emotions collide,
Vivid hues painting what hearts cannot hide.
Each color a cipher, a silent decree,
In the palette of longing, you speak unto me.

With shades of desire, our canvas expands,
Life's brush strokes blend as we take both our hands.
Through greens of envy and blues of the sea,
We dance in the hues of what we could be.

Reds of affection, so bright and so bold,
Whispers of warmth in the stories we've told.
In strokes of deep violet, secrets we keep,
Through mountains of silence, our passions run deep.

With golden sunrises that grace us each day,
We weave through emotions, come what may.
In the colors of time, our journey unclear,
Yet painted in love, we cherish what's dear.

As twilight approaches, the canvas will glow,
In the colors of unspoken, our hearts will still flow.
With each fleeting moment, a masterpiece born,
In vibrant expression, together, we're sworn.

Pulses and Whispers

In the heart's quiet chamber,
Faint echoes start to rise,
With every gentle tremor,
The soul begins to sigh.

Soft murmurs dance in shadows,
Secrets beneath the skin,
Each flicker holds a story,
Of where love has been.

An unseen rhythm beckons,
As twilight's hush unfolds,
In the meeting of our gazes,
A fire slowly molds.

The pulse of life grows stronger,
In whispers shared anew,
A tether forms between us,
A bond both deep and true.

With each heart's secret flutter,
We paint a tale divine,
In the depths of our longing,
A beautiful design.

A Canvas of Desire

Brush strokes paint the silence,
Colors vibrant and bold,
With every stroke of longing,
A canvas soon unfolds.

Dreams mingled with the daylight,
Hues of passion collide,
Amidst the trails of whispers,
Our hearts cannot hide.

Each shade a soft reflection,
Of moments yet to come,
In galleries of yearning,
We find where we belong.

The palette holds our secrets,
In vivid shades we trust,
Creating visions timeless,
In love's embrace, we must.

As layers blend together,
The masterpiece is cast,
A timeless work of art,
A passion built to last.

Yearning in the Moonlight

Underneath the silver beams,
Desires spark and glow,
Bathed in gentle luminescence,
Our feelings start to flow.

Soft whispers fill the evening,
As stars begin to twinkle,
In the hush of night, we linger,
Where hearts begin to wrinkle.

Each glance ignites a longing,
In shadows deep and wide,
With every breath, the world fades,
In love we want to bide.

The moon, a silent witness,
To all our hidden dreams,
In its glow, we find our story,
Woven in silver seams.

Yearning speaks in silences,
In midnight's sweet embrace,
Together we shall wander,
In this enchanted space.

Feelings Like Wildflowers

Amidst the fields of longing,
Colors burst into bloom,
With every fleeting moment,
Our hearts begin to loom.

Wildflowers dance in gardens,
Their fragrance fills the air,
Each petal tells a secret,
Of love beyond compare.

In the gentle wind they sway,
A symphony of grace,
With whispers of affection,
In nature's warm embrace.

Each bloom a soft reminder,
Of feelings rich and true,
In the wildness of our hearts,
A love forever new.

So let us roam the meadows,
Where wildflowers reside,
In their beauty, we'll discover,
The love we cannot hide.

Visions of Tomorrow's Embrace.

In the dawn of dreams that gleam,
Hope unfurls like gentle streams.
Whispers of fate dance in light,
Painting futures bold and bright.

Stars align in cosmic play,
Guiding hearts along the way.
Every step is filled with grace,
As we find our rightful place.

In the warmth of twilight's glow,
Time reveals what we should know.
With each heartbeat, visions rise,
Shattering the darkened skies.

Together we shall boldly stride,
Into the unknown, side by side.
Holding dreams that never fade,
In this journey, unafraid.

As the moonlight softly weaves,
A tapestry of love believes.
Visions of tomorrow's grace,
Embrace us in a sweet chase.

Embers of Desire

Flickering flames begin to wake,
In the heart, a tender ache.
Whispers carried on the breeze,
Ignite the depths, a soul's tease.

Starlit nights hold secrets close,
In the silence, love engrossed.
Every glance, a spark ignites,
In the shadows, endless flights.

Passions swirl in smoky bands,
Two entwined, electric hands.
Lost in dreams where shadows play,
Embers glow, they light the way.

Desires bloom like wildflowers,
In the stillness, love empowers.
With each kiss, the world ignites,
Burning softly through the nights.

In the dark, a flame does spark,
Two hearts dance within the dark.
Embers glow, and we ignite,
Chasing dreams into the night.

Heart's Whisper

In the stillness, soft and clear,
Heart's lullabies we long to hear.
Tales of love woven in breath,
Whispers echo, conquering death.

Every heartbeat tells a tale,
In silence, we will never fail.
Guided by the light within,
Emotions flow, like gentle wind.

In the shadows, fears may creep,
Yet the heart will ever leap.
Knowing that we are but guides,
Through the waves where love abides.

Close your eyes, and feel the way,
Trust the whispers night and day.
For within, a truth does bloom,
Lighting paths, dispelling gloom.

United hearts, we find our voice,
In the quiet, we rejoice.
Heart's whispers urge us to dare,
In this bond, we are laid bare.

Flames in the Night

Dancing shadows flicker bright,
Calling forth the stars alight.
In the silence, laughter flows,
As the warmth of passion glows.

Through the dark, a flicker plays,
Painting dreams in fiery rays.
Every moment, wild and free,
In the depths, just you and me.

HEartbeats echo in the space,
Time stands still in love's embrace.
With every spark, we feel alive,
In this fire, our spirits thrive.

Flames igniting hopes anew,
Lighting paths for me and you.
In this night, we soar and glide,
Together on this passionate ride.

As the dawn begins to break,
We will feel the earth awake.
Yet the embers will remain,
In our souls, a sweet refrain.

Serenade in Bloom

In the garden where dreams grow,
Petals whisper secrets low.
Sunlight dances through the trees,
While the heart sways in the breeze.

Colors splash in sweet delight,
Nature's canvas, pure and bright.
Every bloom a tale to tell,
In a world where love can dwell.

Songs of birds fill the air,
Echoing a tender prayer.
Joyful laughter weaves a thread,
Binding moments softly said.

As twilight hugs the fading day,
Stars in silence start to play.
In this serenade of night,
Hope unfurls its wings in flight.

Tomorrow's promise gently stirs,
In the heart, where longing purrs.
With every bloom, we find a chance,
To taste the sweetness of romance.

Cinders of Unforgettable Nights

Underneath the velvet skies,
Whispers linger, love's soft sighs.
Fires crackle, shadows blend,
Moments cherished, time won't end.

Starlit dances, hearts entwined,
Secrets shared, our souls aligned.
Laughter sparkles, wine's embrace,
In the warmth of passion's grace.

Through the haze of smoky air,
Memories flow with tender care.
Every glance ignites a spark,
In the depths of night so dark.

As embers fade, the dawn will call,
Yet the magic won't dissolve.
In these cinders, warmth remains,
Resonating through our veins.

Unforgettable, we will tread,
In this path where dreams are bred.
With a heartbeat, love ignites,
In the glow of unforgettable nights.

The Poetry of Touch

Fingers trace a gentle line,
In the silence, all is fine.
Skin to skin, our worlds collide,
In this moment, love's our guide.

Every brush ignites a flame,
Whispered words, no need for names.
In the quiet, hearts express,
In this dance of sweet caress.

Textures tell a silent tale,
In the hush, our breaths inhale.
With each sigh, the universe,
Wraps us in this tender verse.

The warmth between us holds so tight,
Guiding stars throughout the night.
In a world where words can flee,
Your touch, my only poetry.

As the dawn begins to rise,
In your arms, the truth lies.
Language fades, yet love endures,
In the poetry of touch, we're sure.

Shattered Silence

In the stillness, echoes roam,
Filling spaces, far from home.
Whispers linger in the dark,
Every heartbeat leaves a mark.

Cracks of silence start to show,
Hidden truths begin to flow.
Voices tremble, shadows creep,
In the depths where secrets sleep.

Tears like raindrops fall and blend,
In the chaos, we may mend.
Fragments glimmer, light breaks through,
From the shards, a new hue grew.

With each shard, a story told,
Bravery found in the bold.
Shattered silence, yet we stand,
In the beauty of the grand.

From the broken, strength is born,
In the night, we greet the dawn.
Embracing all that life unveils,
In shattered silence, love prevails.

Radiant Longing

In the glow of the evening sky,
Whispers of dreams drift by.
Each star a flicker of hope,
Guiding my heart to cope.

Fleeting moments in the night,
Breathless under soft moonlight.
With every glimmering glance,
A chance for a timeless dance.

Crimson colors paint the dawn,
Promises of love reborn.
Through shadows, I seek the light,
Chasing visions, taking flight.

Silent echoes fill the air,
Longing hearts, a fragile pair.
Every beat, a soft refrain,
Together through joy and pain.

As the sun begins to rise,
Hope awakens in the skies.
With radiant hues I long,
To sing my heart's own song.

Tides of Affection

Waves crash gently on the shore,
Each tide whispers tales of yore.
In the dance of sand and sea,
Your love flows deep inside me.

Fluttering leaves, a soft breeze,
Moments shared bring me to ease.
With every sunset, colors blend,
In your arms, I find my mend.

Stars align on velvet nights,
Guiding hearts, glowing lights.
In each ripple, each caress,
I feel the warmth of your finesse.

The ocean's breath, a sweet embrace,
In this vast, enchanted space.
We ride the waves, hand in hand,
Together, we understand.

Tides may shift and seasons change,
Yet our bond will not be strange.
In this journey, love's reflection,
Forever in this connection.

Boundless Yearnings

In the stillness of the night,
Yearnings rise, a silent flight.
Every heartbeat intertwined,
Whispers of the heart aligned.

Moments linger, dreams entwine,
In this space, the stars align.
With the dawn, we chase the light,
Boundless love feels ever right.

Beyond the mountains, oceans wide,
In your eyes, I deeply confide.
Every glance, a promise made,
In this trust, I will not fade.

Through every laugh and tear we share,
The world dissolves, stripped bare.
In each encounter, hearts ignite,
Boundless dreamers chase the night.

With every step along this road,
Together we shall share the load.
In the silence, hear the song,
Eternal love, where we belong.

Silk and Storm

Soft as silk, yet fierce like storm,
Your love—an ever-changing form.
In the calm, our hearts reside,
In the tempest, side by side.

Gentle whispers, tender glow,
Breaching waves, our passions flow.
Through thunder, chaos, winds that wail,
In each other, we prevail.

Stormy nights, a rousing fight,
But in your arms, all feels right.
Every clash, a spark ignites,
In the dark, our love unites.

Silken threads woven in dreams,
Every shadow softly gleams.
Through the wild, we navigate,
Together, we will radiate.

With each storm, I find my peace,
In your gaze, all troubles cease.
Bound by silk and tempest bold,
A love story yet to be told.

Harmonies of Euphoria

In dreams we dance, light as air,
Whispers of joy everywhere,
Colors swirl, a vivid blend,
In this moment, joy transcends.

Laughter rings, a melody sweet,
With every heartbeat, we feel complete,
Time stands still, in this embrace,
Lost in the magic of this space.

Twinkling stars in the midnight sky,
Echo our hopes as they soar high,
A symphony plays, soft and clear,
In harmony, we have no fear.

Golden rays of the morning sun,
Chase away shadows, we have won,
Together we rise, our spirits free,
In joyful union, you and me.

With every laugh, a new refrain,
In this euphoria, we feel no pain,
Hand in hand, through life we roam,
In the melody, we find our home.

Heartbeats in Unison

Two souls collide, a vibrant spark,
In the silence, we leave our mark,
Rhythm flows through every vein,
A symphony of joy, not in vain.

With every touch, our spirits ignite,
In the twilight, hearts feel light,
Together we face the stormy weather,
Our pulse is strong, we are tethered.

Moments shared beneath the stars,
With whispered dreams, we'll heal our scars,
In the night, our secrets spill,
Wrapped in love, we feel the thrill.

A heartbeat's song, like a lullaby,
In your gaze, I learn to fly,
With every breath, the world fades away,
As we dance through life's grand ballet.

Bound in rhythm, our futures align,
Each heartbeat echoes, truly divine,
In this unison, love will thrive,
Together, our spirits come alive.

Labyrinths of Affection

In winding paths, we find our way,
Through twisted turns, come what may,
Every corner holds a story true,
In this maze, my heart finds you.

Soft whispers echo through the night,
Lost in affection, pure and bright,
Each step we take, hand in hand,
In this labyrinth, love will stand.

Through shadowed halls, our laughter sings,
In the chaos, joy it brings,
Winding pathways of sweet desire,
In our hearts, we fuel the fire.

With every turn, we shed our fears,
In this haven, we dry our tears,
Together we forge our own way through,
In the labyrinth, it's me and you.

The exit awaits with open arms,
But for now, we embrace its charms,
In every moment, love we'll weave,
In this maze of affection, we believe.

A Tapestry of Ecstasy

Threads of color, rich and bright,
Woven with whispers of pure delight,
In every strand, a tale unfolds,
Of passion and dreams, of hearts turned bold.

Intertwined with laughter and pain,
Each stitch binds us, in joy, in rain,
In this tapestry, our hearts we share,
Colors meld in the open air.

Moments shimmer like golden thread,
In this fabric, our hopes are bred,
Layer by layer, we stitch our fate,
In the ecstasy, we resonate.

From dawn till dusk, we create a scene,
In vibrant hues of love evergreen,
Through trials and triumphs, a story stays,
In this grand tapestry, the soul plays.

With every weave, our dreams entwine,
A work of art, through love, divine,
In this creation, forever we'll be,
A tapestry of ecstasy.

Liquid Dreams

Drifting on a silver stream,
Whispers of a distant dream.
Stars are twinkling, softly gleam,
Floating through a midnight beam.

Ripples painting tales untold,
In this world where hearts unfold.
Crimson skies and blue of gold,
Drenched in warmth, a love so bold.

Waves of passion wash the shore,
Every moment begs for more.
In the water, we explore,
Liquid dreams forever soar.

With each tide, our secrets shared,
In these depths, we are ensnared.
Floating free, no longer scared,
Love's embrace, so well-prepared.

Underneath a willow's shade,
Gentle sounds, our fears do fade.
Time succumbed, we both conveyed,
In tranquility, hearts swayed.

Moments of Breathless Connection

Two souls meet in fleeting time,
Eyes collide, a silent rhyme.
Heartbeat quickens, feels sublime,
In that glance, we climb and climb.

Breathless whispers shared at dusk,
Each moment wrapped in sacred trust.
In your arms, the world combust,
Love igniting, pure and just.

In the stillness, dreams converge,
Hands entwined, emotions surge.
Time stands still, as hearts emerge,
In this space, we both submerge.

Caught between a hope and fear,
Voices soft, we drift near.
In this dance, the truth is clear,
A spark ignited, ever dear.

Bright horizons beckon us,
In the quiet, amid the fuss.
Every glance is thrilling, thus,
In our love, we learn to trust.

Velvety Embrace

Underneath the velvet skies,
Laughter echoes, love complies.
In your gaze, a sweet surprise,
Wrapped in warmth, where freedom lies.

Silken threads that weave us close,
In this warmth, we love the most.
Every heartbeat, every boast,
In your arms, I feel engrossed.

Gentle winds, a soft caress,
In your whispered words, I guess.
Moments shared, we feel both blessed,
In this bond, we find our rest.

Crimson blush and midnight deep,
Together we no longer weep.
In this embrace, our spirits leap,
Heaven's promise ours to keep.

Velvet nights, a lover's tune,
Underneath the silver moon.
In our hearts, a sweet monsoon,
Let love's chorus start soon.

The Language of Fire

Flames dance where passion ignites,
Each flicker a story invites.
Heat of longing, fierce delights,
In the darkness, love unites.

Crimson embers softly glow,
Whispers of a love we know.
In the fire, our spirits flow,
Together in this ardent show.

Every spark a promise made,
In the blaze, our fears do fade.
With each breath, our hearts cascades,
In this warmth, we are not swayed.

Burning bright, our souls collide,
Through the flames, we take the ride.
Lost in the heat, we confide,
In this dance, we now abide.

From ashes, new dreams arise,
In this blaze, there are no lies.
Lost in warmth, where beauty lies,
The language of fire never dies.

Milton Keynes UK
Ingram Content Group UK Ltd.
UKHW020233230824
447326UK00007B/43